F.L.Y. fully love yourself

fully love yourself

audrey ronette griffin m.a.ed.

F.L.Y.

fully love yourself

audrey ronette griffin m.a.ed.

F.L.Y. fully love yourself

introduction..4
fragile 5
dating 45
healing to f.l.y..77

F.L.Y. fully love yourself

introduction

Married 20 years. Together 22. More. Than. Half. My life. Gone. I will rise again. This time with more wisdom and love. I will F.L.Y. high, loving myself fully as the light I was called to be.

I am so grateful for my mother, who wiped my tears and supported me in every way. I am so grateful for Tai, who literally held my hand through every step of the process. I am so grateful for Aisha, for always reminding me of how beautiful I am. I am so grateful for Marissa, for always being there and rooting for me. I am so grateful for Rhonda, for your wisdom. I am so grateful for Lauren, for listening to me rant about moon child shit. I am grateful for my brother Roney and his wife Linda, for making sure that they were present and supportive for me and my children. I am so grateful for June, you are my family. I am so grateful for my brothers Junie and Seth, for supporting me. I am so grateful for Scott, for pushing me to follow through with my dreams. Last and certainly not least, I am forever grateful for my children, Vanessa, Alan, Aubrey and Adrian Jr. None of it was in vein, because without him, there would be no you, and you four are more than worth it ALL.

F.L.Y. fully love yourself

fragile

F.L.Y. fully love yourself

i can't wait to see you, he

said.

me either,

i said.

get here as fast as you

can. ok.

i booked my flight. after

a layover in ireland, that

was beautiful,

i told myself,

i must return.

i then arrived in Spain.

F.L.Y. fully love yourself

i saw an email...

when does your wife get here?

i ignored it.

not possible.

in another country?

c'mon...

denial.

he sent me an email:

i can't wait to spend

the rest of my life with you.

i should pretended not to see

the email from her.

he means what he says to me. right?

besides,

i'm not ready to be the other woman.

F.L.Y. fully love yourself

it was good...

that was part of the problem I presume.

it was always good.

it would make me forget momentarily.

only to later awaken to the reality of the truth.

do people stay longer than they should?

not for the kids,

maybe for how the kids got here?

soul ties...

need to be cut.

the longer they are,

the stronger the chord.

sever it!

F.L.Y. fully love yourself

we argued about devices.

i am on mine too much he says.

what am I searching for?

something

is

missing.

i know what its like to not

be preoccupied when you

are in good company.

why is he not good company to me?

i feel the stare of his evil eye.

i decide to turn over

and go to sleep.

F.L.Y. fully love yourself

i'm sorry.

me too.

takes a tour.

takes photos.

takes a selfie (usie)

i'm shocked.

he compromised.

i compromised.

had a few dranks.

yes dranks!

we had fun.

momentary bliss...

we went for a run on the water.

my soul felt amazing.

he said he felt good too.

i wanted to feel more of this good.

i wanted to paddle board.

he didn't have time.

i did,

he went to work.

i went.

he went back to the room.

here.

we.

are.

again.

a disconnect.

a work thing... again,

but i understood.

i always understood.

F.L.Y. fully love yourself

i wish my kids were here.

as i watch the team celebrate

with their families,

they looked happy.

not sure why,

but the facade i no longer

wanted to entertain.

he didn't like

me being me,

because that often

meant to him

they'd like me more.

he always said,

he never wanted to share me.

whatever that meant.

oh well.

headed home now,

victory at hand.

they won the gold.

we lost...

in love.

F.L.Y. fully love yourself

silence.

i don't mind silence.

absence.

that's what scares me.

you can be here.

and

not

be

here.

F.L.Y. fully love yourself

we moved closer to his work,

to see each other more.

an hour commute

was now 17 minutes.

but somehow,

we managed,

to see each other...

less.

less is not more.

F.L.Y. fully love yourself

flowers for the lady.

i smiled,

but i didn't appreciate them.

i felt something was wrong,

really wrong.

who likes to get flowers

when something is wrong?

flowers

can't

fix

this.

i didn't know he meant it,

we each get a certain amount,

but we don't have to get each other anything.

this was confusing...

we've always gotten each other something,

even if it was small.

so i thought he must be surprising me.

i spent my portion on him.

he got mad i got him something.

then...

the last minute gift.

19 years and this was

the best you could do?

i have never felt so

insulted.

not the gift,

but the lack of thought.

keep your gift card, that wasn't even 10 percent of what we had.

i thought to myself.

instead... i smiled

and said thank you.

the kids were happy.

facades continue...

it dawned on me looking back...

maybe he spent it on her.

F.L.Y. fully love yourself

it's New Years!

we can't screw this up, right?

we are invited to a party.

dinner with the family,

then partying after, couldn't be more perfect.

plot twist...

"hey what do you want for dinner tonight?"

"who cares. why should I be excited about celebrating with you and this shitty marriage"

whoa. wait. what?!?

i called him, immediately, because that had to be a mistake.

it wasn't.

he was being mean again.

the old me would've continued to try and fix it.

for some reason this time.

i didn't want to fix it tonight.

fuck him.

got dressed.

left.

went to dinner and to a party with with my girl.

i smiled through it.

gave the excuses as to why he wasn't there.

as the moments passed and midnight got closer.

i. felt. empty.

it was different

not kissing him this year.

suddenly I wanted to be home.

i called.

everyone was somewhere different.

it. wasn't. the. same.

F.L.Y. fully love yourself

we need help.

we need help..

we need help!!!

no response.

get out!!!!!

i cried.

i cant live like this

any. more.

he went back

to sleep.

i went downstairs.

F.L.Y. fully love yourself

morning rises.

a new day.

he picked a fight.

so he could have a

reason to leave.

i egged the fight on,

to give him a reason to leave.

he said i am leaving you.

i said why?

we need to get help.

he argued and said,

he'd be back for the rest of his things later.

as he walked past me to get to his closet,

he had his bag in his hand.

i felt the anger,

the hurt,

the sadness,

why didn't we know how to love one another?

clearly we loved one another.

a still voice inside of me said,

let.

him.

go.

i fought that voice with my ego.

i lost.

egos always lose.

F.L.Y. fully love yourself

you calculated your every move.

i responded from my heart,

but you ripped it apart.

i found 7 others.

7 others!

cleveland,

miami,

toronto,

new jersey,

3 in chicago!

i didn't know interviews

were being held for my position.

F.L.Y. fully love yourself

it was late...

i thought everyone was sleep.

my daughters caught me,

caught me crying.

mom you are always here for us,

let us be here for you.

they hugged me.

we cried in my bathroom.

12:30 am.

F.L.Y. fully love yourself

what if i leave?

why do i have to stay?

he should come be with the kids.

half way out of the state

i.

turned.

around.

my babies.

there must be someone else...

no way a man leaves his family to be alone.

she didn't think she destroyed my family

i couldn't prove it,

ig did.

the ring he had my daughter approve,

said it was for someone else,

right there on her finger,

on her friends page.

they had been dating

since 2014.

it's 2016.

thanks to social media

for putting it on front street.

it didn't end... the only thing i've ever trusted.

it was right, once again.

my gut.

i'm going to file, he said.

why? i said.

i'm going to file.

why are we doing this?

what is our reason?

he said he didn't care what i told people the reason was.

he was filing.

he hung up.

i cried.

facade over.

F.L.Y. fully love yourself

my son answered the door,

he hadn't gone to school that day.

i came to the door.

my heart sank.

this was really happening.

i

got.

served.

F.L.Y. fully love yourself

i hadn't eaten.

i couldn't.

i ate just enough to function.

i stayed in bed most days.

cried about failing.

failing in my marriage.

failing to my kids.

i talked to one of our mutual friends daily.

a friend i fought to keep because he didn't like him.

he thought males couldn't be friends with females.

not true.

he teased his wife to me,

called them both names at

several points and we fought 6 years about him,

because i would not give him up as a friend.

then they went into business together,

he got over it, when he thought they could make money together.

i cried with this friend. i prayed with him. he gave me hope,

that with God anything was possible.

he ended up being in his wedding to the paramour.

what God does he serve i asked?

we are no longer friends.

who used who?

clout chaser.

F.L.Y. fully love yourself

my friends were going on vacation.

you should come, they said.

i didn't want to.

my mom convinced me to not only go,

but she would pay for my trip.

my sitter watched my kids for free.

i had no money.

he was giving me $100 a day

to live on

with four kids.

while he'd take out $400-500 at a time from an atm.

i needed this vacation,

more than i knew.

i was waisting away physically,

spiritually i had nothing left to give.

it was a quick and beautiful trip.

i love my friends.

for laughing with me,

having dinners,

dancing,

swimming,

and reading books about the stars.

then it was back home,

to face the ugly truth.

he had an epiphany...

he understood why God hated divorce.

i tried to be excited.

told him i was happy for him.

but as much as i cared,

i felt myself giving up.

F.L.Y. fully love yourself

i had tickets to a concert

and came across a cutie on ig.

i guess we had friends in common.

i was bold, since i now accepted this divorce

and slid in the dm.

no shame.

we talked.

he came with me.

we went back to his place,

and well lets just say...

that was my first and last

netflix and chill.

fun though.

F.L.Y. fully love yourself

on my drive home,

i talked to my girl all about it.

we giggled like two teenagers....

as i walked in the house and

continued to laugh about

this crazy fun night.

lights were out.

kids were sleep.

i tip toed to my room,

then i wanted a snack.

went back down to the kitchen

and realized he was on the couch.

oh shit...

did he hear any of that?

after living in hotels for 3 months...

he.

came.

home.

F.L.Y. fully love yourself

we went to the movies.

we went out to eat.

we went to the kids games.

he invited me to his games.

it was a glimpse of normal again.

and then...

we

made

love.

but i had my first vision then,

i saw her.

the.

other.

woman.

that night i had a dream,

a very detailed dream

i hardly remember my dreams...

it was my warning.

i knew.

ego stepped in,

you got this.

well I didn't.

she did.

i felt it.

i told him about my dream

he asked with interest.

as if his ego was pleased.

he tried to contain it,

but i saw.

the only thing he convinced me

of during that conversation was when he said,

no one deserves to be by my side

when i make it, other than you.

no. other. woman.

you were there with me, through it all.

i believed him.

F.L.Y. fully love yourself

i drove him to the airport.

here we were,

another move.

my kids were excited.

they wanted to go to

the sunshine state.

i thought this could be

the change we need.

new environment,

back to family.

texts went back and forth,

lets get this dog,

lets get this house,

and then...

it stopped.

i saw an email,

they were looking for

an apartment together.

surely it was her.

my gut.

right again.

i really wanted for it to be wrong.

but 6 people cant fit in a 2 bedroom condo.

F.L.Y. fully love yourself

he came home,

like nothing happened.

he got a condo up the street.

and moved out

i was confused.

my spirit wasn't though.

he stayed with us most nights.

i could count how many nights he was at that apartment.

he convinced me,

he just needed space,

to think.

i knew he was lying.

but.

my.

family.

july 4 2015.

a hotel lobby,

she. was. there.

a conversation she referred to me as his ex-wife.

i wanted to slap the shit out of her,

but my daughter was present.

the home wrecker threw him under the bus...

why did she want him?

i told her to be a woman, walk away until we finish this said here business.

as she got her room cut off from her 70 year old fiancé,

who kept calling her while we were talking, he found out he paid for her trip to see him,

i wanted to plummet this trifling becky.

my daughter said she wasn't worth it.

the jail time.

she was right.

we went up to the room,

he wouldn't let us in.

he didn't let my son let us in,

he called security on Us instead.

a coward.

my daughter and i were stranded until 4 am,

as We sat in that lobby bathroom,

my ego got out of the driver seat.

survival mode kicked in.

called my lawyers.

its back on.

moving forward with the divorce.

somewhat relieved,

but angry.

here i am stuck.

one day while working out,

with my trainer.

he said, why are you stuck?

you can go too...

and i asked my lawyers

to get it done.

the judge cleared us to leave.

i packed so quick,

quicker than a ny minute.

on our way...

home.

F.L.Y. fully love yourself

support

and love.

that's what motivated the 12 hour straight drive.

we got around people who loved us,

dinner with family.

dinner with friends.

meditation.

prayer.

Gods word for strength...

change the way i saw myself...

i'm not just a wife and mother.

i was a chosen being, by God, to be here to fulfill my purpose.

i started living from the heart of myself.

love was my cure.

love myself.

love my family.

love my kids.

i could only imagine what it felt like for them,

my dad was always there for me.

they had to deal with the unthinkable.

an un-present parent,

by choice.

i couldn't fathom that rejection.

man i had to love my kids hard!

F.L.Y. fully love yourself

this

is

happening.

he

has

moved

on.

i will honor my vows,

until they are no longer.

date they say,

i

said

no.

i'm

working

on

me.

F.L.Y. fully love yourself

running.

because it is healing,

not because i need to lose weight.

the divorce diet had taken care of that.

plus it was thanksgiving.

a first,

by choice,

with

out

him.

F.L.Y. fully love yourself

back and forth,

back and forth.

tired of creating a bill,

but then becky emails me.

had the nerve to tell

me i wasn't a good wife,

nor mother.

i wasn't offended by the wife part,

but the mother part,

bitch.

do.

not.

come.

for.

me.

i will die for mine.

my childhood friends called her

email bitch.

yep

petty.

we spoke for the first time in months.

our youngest was acting out,

as they say.

my middle child was crying a lot,

and my oldest son

was trying to cope.

my oldest, couldn't figure out

how we didn't work through this.

we had seen worse.

and why he was wearing

the wedding band from our marriage.

there was a lot of unspoken

hurt in that brief convo.

becky then made it so

he could only email.

no text,

no calls,

just email.

email bitch.

F.L.Y. fully love yourself

it's time.

time to seal the deal.

he kept fidgeting,

i know that look.

hell i know him better than anyone.

and when he did that thing with his hand.

oh lord...

do i show him pictures and videos

of becky with the other players, to try and save him?

nah.

i'm over it.

go lay in your bed.

besides if we didn't agree today,

this was what the judge was going to rule.

i wasn't even going to get dissipation,

but he lied to the judge,

got caught...

and he had to write a check to me by friday.

then it was over.

i got back on a plane to ny.

he flew to his game in boston.

he tore his achilles that night.

guess karma doesn't miss any address,

and she was just getting started on him.

F.L.Y. fully love yourself

it was my friends 40th birthday.

i thought wow.

i'm divorced

and I am about to be 40 in 6 months.

sure didn't plan this.

but guess what?

i had fun that night.

i danced,

i ate and

i drank.

and after 22 years...

i.

was.

free.

F.L.Y. fully love yourself

basketball games...

my son one game short to county center.

he received so many awards.

my daughter won state.

and federation.

we.

were.

on.

a.

roll.

my kids continued to shine.

all their tears, so they could see rainbows.

and me...

i brought my first house,

my first car,

all in my name.

it had been 40 years and i never had

a house, or car in my name...

it felt good and i took pictures.

through it all, i didn't fail at marriage.

i graduated. graduated and moved my life in a different direction.

forward.

i wanted to live and be brave again.

and guess who started dating?

me.

F.L.Y. fully love yourself

dating

F.L.Y. fully love yourself

such a big city...

bad date,

great date.

who to date?

keep to date?

instantly attracted to fun!

time to explore!

living life,

on my terms.

one.

day.

at.

a.

time.

F.L.Y. fully love yourself

called my bff,

since 2nd grade.

she is my wind beneath my wings.

if i ever needed a friend...

she's had my back since,

well since i could remember.

i'm divorced girl,

let's celebrate!

guess what we did?

went out to eat. lol

sorry i'm not experienced.

i have no clue

what to do.

yet.

F.L.Y. fully love yourself

the culture,

the food,

the fuckboi's,

texts on read,

facetime,

drinks,

day parties,

rosters,

uber rides at 4am...

welcome.

to.

the.

single.

life.

nyc.

F.L.Y. fully love yourself

he looked at me

with dreamy eyes,

i looked at him

like just one night.

F.L.Y. fully love yourself

can you tell a lot

about a person from their friends?

i think so.

his friend was nice,

but he couldn't stop staring.

so i chose him instead.

F.L.Y. fully love yourself

we went to dinner.

i was inebriated by the main course.

was i being a lady?

didn't care.

just wanted to have fun.

he drove my car

i was in no condition to.

i trusted him

and guess what

we made it to part 2.

part 2 was a club in BK.

it was a ton of fun!

couldn't keep my hands to myself.

then back to the hotel.

what the hell was i doing?

i thought to myself,

i'm not like this.

definitely not the route i want to take.

everyone keeps saying your free,

have fun!

so, fuck it, became my motto,

and i did just that.

F.L.Y. fully love yourself

no orgasm,

no oohs and aahs,

just something to do.

yeah time to go.

once is enough,

i'm not bout this life.

F.L.Y. fully love yourself

single saturday's.

the idea that it was

all fun and games at 18.

what is it like now at 40?

haha

just as fun!

if not funners!!!

yes

funners.

everything you snuck to do

as a kid,

was now ok,

because

you're

grown.

F.L.Y. fully love yourself

cupid.

she gave him my number.

she knew him.

i had a new found crush.

hadn't had a crush in a while.

actually knew of him for a while,

but she liked him first.

i didn't.

now I was single,

looking with different eyes.

i was like, are you sure?

she was like, absolutely!

ok I will talk to him.

F.L.Y. fully love yourself

him: hello.

me: hey its me!

me: duh of course you know, i called.

i remember nothing after that...

worst first conversation ever.

a few texts later...

fade.

to.

black.

back to the drawing board.
taking this time for myself.
learning myself.
about a month later...
minding my business.
depositing checks.
someone saw me
the next day I returned.
she asked were you here yesterday?
i replied yes.
he inquired about me,
she showed me a photo.
me: before we go any further in info, is he tall?
her: yes
i got his name.
hit him up on fb.
several days later
he replied and sent his number.
we had
conversations that lasted for hours.
he interrupted his sleep for me,
he wanted to know about me,
he was so into me,
we laughed.
we learned.
we explored.
it had the makings of something real.
so i thought...

F.L.Y. fully love yourself

first date was breakfast.

i saw him walk in,

he was later than me.

i knew it wasn't going to last,

but i thought...

this could be fun!

our conversations were intense,

in a good way.

it was entertaining.

i learned to laugh again.

and i loved how

he wanted to do whatever i wanted,

but then...

F.L.Y. fully love yourself

they were best friends.

he visited her,

didn't answer his phone.

i know what this is.

this.

is.

not.

what.

i.

want.

F.L.Y. fully love yourself

i tried to leave.

i broke up with him 3 times.

he came back.

he wanted to make me happy,

i think i wanted to be free.

he mentioned marriage to his 'best friend'

who she also begged me not to leave him.

my heart said, he's a good guy.

my spirit said, he's not the one.

so i broke up with him again,

but my ego thought he'd come back again.

he said no.

that bothered me,

i knew i still had lots of work to do.

left him alone,

when i knew he met someone else.

it was only a week later.

so my guess is she was there for a while.

actually wish them the best,

he's not my type,

but it was fun.

just as i thought.

always go with your first instinct.

F.L.Y. fully love yourself

he texted me.

my heart stopped,

i was happy to hear from him.

this time,

the conversation flowed much better.

then it began,

my

new

obsession.

F.L.Y. fully love yourself

first date...
i'm running late.
anticipating
as he waits,
i walk in,
he stands up
to greet me.
i have my heels on,
and he still towers over me.
chocolate and fine!
the hug was everything
lawd help me.
he pulls table out,
so I can sit...
we talked for a couple of hours.
i have never been so interested
in listening to someone in my entire life.
i indulged in every word he said,
as they rolled off of his tongue,
it was divine.
as he mentioned things,
i couldn't help but learn how much we had in common.
i thought, is this what people mean
when you meet someone, and wouldn't have to change,
because y'all literally like the same things?
my attention i was giving,
was definitely not minimum wage.
i woulda promoted him and gave him a 401k!

F.L.Y. fully love yourself

before i kissed you for the first time,

i looked into your eyes,

i didn't know how you would taste,

the tension had been rising,

we shared lovely stories,

funny stories,

ambitious stories,

but a moment came,

something rose in me,

like never before,

as i reached over the table,

and gently whisked your

handsome face in my hand,

and damn...

there it was,

a storm beneath my skin,

the hairs on my neck stood,

i had goosebumps everywhere,

it was...

pure flames.

F.L.Y. fully love yourself

when she met him,

he said what she felt.

he worded

what she thought.

suddenly all that was

inside of her already,

became alive,

an awakening.

F.L.Y. fully love yourself

i didn't feel well that morning.
he held my head while
i laid on his chest...
i abruptly got up,
to throw up in the bathroom.
brushed my teeth,
returned to bed.
returned to his chest,
but it made me nauseous to lay down.
he raised me up,
placed himself behind me,
and held me up.
my back to his chest,
as i now laid in between his legs.
he wrapped his arms around me,
he kissed my neck,
and all of a sudden
i was better.
he kissed my head,
i turned to him,
we kissed,
and laid there.
intimately,
quietly.
what wasn't said,
was beautiful.
so pure.
how do i know...
you hear me
when i do not speak.

F.L.Y. fully love yourself

when i lay on you,

we breathe with such synchronicity.

the feeling that we become one,

is unreal.

i made it out of hell,

just so i could feel this heaven.

F.L.Y. fully love yourself

i have always believed

in what i felt,

now i just trust it

more

than

what

i

see.

F.L.Y. fully love yourself

there is a magic

i feel for you,

that i know

i always want.

when the world falls silent,

that's when my love for you is the loudest.

F.L.Y. fully love yourself

when your lips

are pressed against mine,

i get a warm sensation.

a tingling inside,

i don't want to stop.

it tastes so good...

like succulent honey,

better than any food.

F.L.Y. fully love yourself

i'd rather hold hands,

than hold devices.

i want to get lost,

where wifi is weak.

lie and bask in the sun,

where the rum is strong.

the virtual world...

a distraction if you may...

but only until the desire is so unequivocally to

live,

feel,

connect,

and most importantly...

BE.

once again.

F.L.Y. fully love yourself

for the first time

i am thankful for fear,

because i am afraid

of losing someone,

that has no reason

to stay with me,

other than to want to.

F.L.Y. fully love yourself

as i look around the table...

the dressing is being passed,

stories are being shared,

smiles are exchanged.

we stop and catch a glimpse

of one another,

looking into each other's eyes,

as our souls are pouring over

with nothing but love,

and thanksgiving.

F.L.Y. fully love yourself

i lost my balance for you,

and that's ok,

because sometimes when

you lose your balance for love,

out of it comes,

the.

most.

perfect.

alignment.

F.L.Y. fully love yourself

i don't feel incomplete,

in fact I feel whole.

when i found you,

i finally found someone

i wanted to share

my highest form of self with,

and

it

feels

beautiful.

F.L.Y. fully love yourself

you wear the crown in my heart,

because you make my spirit dance.

it dances with such joy.

you're the only one that could have a chance.

touching parts of me i didn't know existed.

i come alive when i'm with you, nope never bored.

with you I always have

the sweet desire for more.

F.L.Y. fully love yourself

you and i are an expression

of the divine love of God.

loving myself, allows me

to love you, unconditionally.

being with you is like

a spiritual awakening.

letting go of the old,

transcending into the new.

a higher self.

coming out of the dark.

not into the light,

but realizing

we.

are.

the.

light.

F.L.Y. fully love yourself

i have never felt anything like that before,

as we gazed into one another eyes...

all i felt was pure love.

i wanted to cry.

he said, you better not be bullshitting me,

i said i'm not,

you couldn't fake what was felt,

on any level.

F.L.Y. fully love yourself

healing to f.l.y.

F.L.Y. fully love yourself

i woke up today,

had a vision so clear,

why is he so evil to me?

how could he show so much hate

towards someone he spent half his life with?

we laughed often,

we laughed hard,

we played,

we dated,

we did all the things you do to keep love alive,

we were real life goals, on paper.

then a soft whisper...

until he meets the demon within him,

he will continue to try and slay them in me.

i pray he finds out he can not,

and he looks within to do the work.

self healing.

i will still pray for him.

i questioned my demons.

i wanted to know all of them,

intimately.

so i can know

how to defuse them.

F.L.Y. fully love yourself

the journey to finding love

begins at home.

home is where your heart is,

and your heart is

in between the chest cavity.

yes.

this.

you.

are.

your.

home.

F.L.Y. fully love yourself

loving someone my entire adult life,

it was a constant compromise.

i didn't know what it meant,

how, or to what capacity,

to love myself.

i had to learn

and in order to do so,

i had to unlearn.

F.L.Y. fully love yourself

codependency was my clutch.

i never knew how to be self-soothing.

my teacher was scared of loss.

so she clinched, clanged,

and made no quorums,

with anything, or

anyone, she loved.

i

had

to

unlearn

co-dependency,

to gain

the unconditional

freedom in love.

F.L.Y. fully love yourself

as a clinger...
i had let him cling my neck,
i had let him cling my arm,
i had let him throw me
against a wall.
the force made a hole that night.
i questioned how was this love?
how do i get thrown against a wall,
because of his indiscretions?
but i didn't sit in this for too long.
my first instinct was to fix it.
hurry... call a handyman.
before
the
kids
get
home.
because the aesthetics of our
brand new model home,
was more important than
his mistress calling me.
memory triggers.

F.L.Y. fully love yourself

as certain memories cross my mind,

i wanted to hug my younger self.

i read all of the quotes,

and sayings about love...

none of theses were in the description.

but there had to be some love,

because it was held together

for.

so.

long.

F.L.Y. fully love yourself

when you come across

a definition,

one that defines your truth,

you take a deep breath...

you realize,

you are not crazy,

you are not insane,

you are in fact,

with out a single doubt,

love.

it's just that you loved

a narcissist.

and your only downfall

was thinking,

he knew how to love you back.

F.L.Y. fully love yourself

you can't change someone.

you can't change someone.

you can't change someone.

you will realize and

come to peace with this,

when you begin to do the work

to change yourself.

it.

is.

hard.

F.L.Y. fully love yourself

when i think of love...

i think of a feeling,

an indescribable feeling.

one that is hard to word,

but i know love is not,

griping someones neck

until they are unconscious,

then apologizing for it.

love is not dragging

someone across a lawn

when they are pregnant,

or out of patio doors,

putting bruises all over their body,

as a child holds their legs,

to tell them to stop hurting their mom.

no.

more.

i'm sorry's.

that.

is.

not.

love.

F.L.Y. fully love yourself

love is forgiving.

love is standing beside someone,

no matter how weak your legs are.

love is support.

love is keeping a family together,

when tough times try to pull them apart.

because in the high profile world,

family is all you've got.

love is respect.

when you lose those things.

those very priceless things,

what do you gain?

i'm not sure yet.

i'm still trying to figure it out.

F.L.Y. fully love yourself

22 years.

twenty two years.

done!

and after 22 years,

i realized...

i only watched that show

because you did.

i haven't seen that show since.

now i watch comedy.

turns out...

i like to laugh more.

F.L.Y. fully love yourself

hey love.

what do you like?

what don't you like?

what are your goals?

what are your dreams?

ask yourself...

why?

because you no longer

have to compromise.

and when you learn these things about yourself,

learn not to compromise them.

not at all, but be who you are.

your people...

your true people...

will love these things about you.

they are the ones that will show up.

these people,

they

are

your

true

tribe.

went to a cooking class.

i enjoyed learning

how to cook a new meal.

turns out...

i do like to cook,

but i prefer hands on teaching.

all these years

i despised my kitchen,

loathed the grocery store.

all i wanted was

some good ol' fashion teaching,

but i still loath grocery shopping.

ha!

i mean...

those isles,

those carts,

those lines,

the loading,

the unloading,

the putting everything away at home.

Jeffery!!???

F.L.Y. fully love yourself

finally started doing yoga

on a regular basis,

that is.

bending,

breathing,

being.

very soothing to my soul.

a self love,

my body,

my mind,

my spirit,

very much needed.

namaste.

F.L.Y. fully love yourself

received a visit

from my aunt.

you know,

my moms best friend...

she knew me before.

before. all. of. this.

before marriage,

before kids,

before the "glam" life.

she. KNEW. me.

she said...

write your story.

i said me?

she said yes!

i said to myself, wow. ok.

then she said, get back to you!

the Ronette before all of this.

my look was like a deer in headlights.

she said, yes her, that girl was amazing!

i don't know, but something about this conversation resonated with me.

it moved my spirit,

as if to cast out demons of sort.

something was planted in me that day

that continues to grow.

a seed. a seed of my true light and being.

thank you auntie.

F.L.Y. fully love yourself

meditate.

meditate.

meditate on what i'm saying.

people are dying,

babies are crying,

meditate.

meditate.

crack a egg on ya head

and let the yolk drip down,

the yolk drip down,

crack a egg on ya head

and let the yolk drip down,

the yolk drip down...

just some childhood nostalgia,

to remember my childlike heart.

concentrate.

i began remembering.

remembering who SHE was.

i went through old photographs,

found old letters written to me,

from male friends,

from female friends,

describing how amazing i was to them.

i was like daaaaaaammmmmmn...

i was loved.

i loved.

i do know how to love.

drove on the block.

the block used to be hot.

my first race, my first crush, my first fight.

it all went down here.

i walked up to my house,

i saw the window i looked out of everyday...

i dreamed a lot of dreams there.

i was also teased through that window.

my brother and i had an early curfew,

our friends would yell to the window and laugh.

or if our lights were on, they'd

yell to our parents that we were sneaking to be up.

yes. petty. funny. kids.

the sidewalk was still broke...

my dad argued with a neighbor

who kept rolling over the sidewalk there.

she kept parking there.

she's gone and my dad is too.

the azaleas are gone.

the walkway gone.

the iron fence gone.

but the memories...

are still here. in my heart. in me.

shaped who i am.

reminded me who i need to be again...

ME.

we met for tea and coffee.

when i arrived,

he was in a gray sweatshirt and jeans.

he had sandy beach hair,

bright blue eyes.

his smile,

his sarcasm,

were all the same.

it was comforting.

like a walk back to high school...

to where i was me,

he was he,

and we were we.

i said, omg you look the same!

he said, you do too...

but with a hint of housewives of miami!

haha...

we laughed

we caught up.

quickly.

we'll have to meet again soon.

and old friend.

F.L.Y. fully love yourself

when we return to

where we are from,

you remember.

you remember who you are.

i now know like i know

why they say...

never forget where

you came from.

i had forgotten for a long time.

F.L.Y. fully love yourself

i let go of the fact that

i thought i knew what i was doing.

i accepted the detour...

and guess what?

i

no

longer

look

back.

F.L.Y. fully love yourself

and in an instant,

God whispered...

do not rush my love,

do not fret nor worry,

i am working everything out.

all you have to do is believe,

and receive.

keep your eyes on me.

captain of my ship.

He got me.

F.L.Y. fully love yourself

salt baths,

sage,

hot teas,

mediation,

prayer,

love...

I AM.

Made in the USA
Columbia, SC
31 March 2022